Musings of a Contemporary Heart

Korina Tsipoura

BookLeaf Publishing

India | USA | UK

Presentation by *BookLeaf Publishing*

Web: www.bookleafpub.com

E-mail: info@bookleafpub.com

ISBN: 9789363309104

First edition 2024

*May my written words land in your heart and
soul and create ripples of love.*

*May they awaken asleep stories of community
and connectedness that have been squeezed into
conformity's clothes of utopia.*

Soul message

As you go into this work, remember
The baby doesn't stand up and starts walking
perfectly
The process of learning how to walk is
necessary
Falling is necessary
Without falling, the map of walking in the
baby's brain will not be fully drawn

As so, in charting the map of your
self-awareness
Allow yourself to fall
Allow the messiness of the process to take place
Love yourself even more for the courage it takes
to go through it
It is never a perfected process
It requires you to release your expectation to
float to the other side
You may need to navigate the deep murky
waters of your shadow

But as you come through to the other side
Oh, my beauty!
Are there even words to describe your full
embodiment?

Is there a language that can express your felt
experience?

Like a flower, we are in awe of its beauty
we experience it through our senses
So is your coming home
it is witnessed through your energetic radiance

We absorb you
We see you
You are held
You are loved

Remembrance

What a humbling experience to remember the
depth of your soul
What a humbling experience this life is

To come here

In naivety
In awe
In expectation

With childlike enthusiasm

To forget it all
And to remember

To add another prism to your collection of
perceptions and experiences of lifetimes

To live life as it is

In its 3-dimensionality
In its density
In its joy

Yet, always remember who you are
Remember the essence of you

Work-life balance...

Ah, that elusive work-life balance.

Which lunatic invented that term?
Who started this insanity?

Here I am, a mum of two
juggling
home
life
wife
relationships
friendships
children
tantrums
shopping
cooking
household managing
self?
work
integrity
values
business
hustle culture
healing
realisations

systems
patriarchy
school drop-offs
inner work
spiritual life
mother in-law
father wounds
finances
playdates
breastfeeding
cleaning
self-care?

Who has the answer to this illusion of balance?

I was overwhelmed.
Over-worked.
Under-supported.
I was never enough.
This was a losing battle.
One day I crashed… depleted, burnt out.

Withering in between conscious and
unconscious states.

And there I had…
A moment of lucidity
A clear decision to be made.
I was not done with life yet.

But I had to let go of… something…

I let go of the insanity to do it all
I rested in the wisdom of my being

I embraced mess and failure
in ways that mean humanness and life

That was the beginning of my convalescence
putting my pieces together
the journey back to self
back home
a rebirth
a commitment to the path
a renewal of the contract with spirit
a yes to life
a yes to healing
a yes to balance within.

Being

I used to believe that life is a school
We come here to learn

I lived in that search of learning for too long

The search of knowledge
The search of healing
The search of myself

When will I have learned enough, I wondered?
When will I be enough?
When will the lessons finish?
When will I be healed?
When will I live?

Perpetuating cycles of inadequacy…

Until I was fed up
and took a bold step
towards life
living
being

Being…

enough
messy
human
simple
loving
accepting

Living

Present

In life, with life, with me and others

with everydayness

This is the hero
everydayness

Then you know that you live

Not in the big moments only
but the small, the unimportant, the private, the
unseen

Are you enough then?
Are you present then?
Are you being then?

This is your testament to living

Life

A string of events

Silence in between

Motion, movement, flow

The ephemeral of the moment

Stillness

Obstacles, turns, breaks and pauses

A winding path

A narrative of emotions

Stories I tell my self

Stories I heard

Stories other people say

My humanness

Energy

When body and mind are merging

When life pours out of the soul

When I am aligned

Life is lived

Pure consciousness

Growth

Expansion

Divine design

Ode to woman

What is a woman
How misunderstood
In the eternity of time

How she's been pushed and squeezed into
unbearable conformity
The cloak of patriarchy upon her
The fear of her power

Weighing her down with
insecurities of her divine nature
sins of her divine body

But the woman's body is powerful

It holds the key to the mysteries of life

It is the bridge from life to death to rebirth

The woman's body
is not to be left a taboo

It is to be experienced
explored
with reverence

with devotion

A sacred space
A temple

When in tune with her cycles
Inseparable part of nature
Part of life

She can withstand the pressure needed to reach
revolution
She is revolution in her wholeness
In her being

Sovereignty

When she was young
She thought she will change her man
She will dismantle the patriarchy within him
She will teach him

Little did she know
That the patriarchy had to be dissolved within
her first

So, she protested
And shouted
For her freedom
Equality
The respect that was due
She fought for her worth

That young version of her
Needed a voice
And now she had it

But as she went on
The well of satisfaction in her life was not
becoming full
The well of her worth was not swelling
Her not enough-ness was still there plaguing her

She followed the signs

She became that woman
Who doesn't have to prove her worth
Because she embodies it

She doesn't have to fight for her equality
Because she knows her nature

She doesn't need approval for her freedom
Because she is free

Moment to moment
Breath to breath
She reclaimed herself
Reclaimed her wholeness
She grew her own roots
She created her own foundation

She strengthened her spine
Healed her womb
Forged a new path

She wrote a new definition for safety

Ebb and flow

Somewhere along the way
you watered yourself down

The father wound
the childhood conditioning
the fear of being too loud
too eccentric
too playful

not seen
not listened
not loved for who you truly are

You had to be a certain way to be worthy of
attention
to be acknowledged
to be accepted

It rubs off on the fabric of your being
until one day you wake up
and your soul is screaming in discomfort

And you start...

painstakingly plucking bit by bit by bit

layer by layer
until you uncover a self
that resembles a little more
that beautiful child that you faintly remember

Of course there is always more to uncover

But trust me

there is a day

when you finally feel comfortable in your own
skin
the dive into the depths of your soul doesn't
scare you
joy is higher up on the surface

Life smells and feels beautiful
even if you haven't got it all sussed out

The day that you feel down doesn't fully knock
you out
And you are able to live life fully in its ebbs and
flows

Accept it all
the ebb and the flow
Sacred parts of who you are

There is no right or wrong way to get where you
want
You are the way
Stop trying to achieve
Become the achievement
You are your most precious thing
You are your sacred job

Softness

Just a reminder

There is no rush
There is no destination you need to reach

You can rest in the wisdom that
You are exactly where you need to be

Take your time
Take the space you need

Give permission to yourself to linger in the
in-between
The in-between of a decision
The in-between of your thoughts
The liminal space before the action

No rush
The world can wait

Know that it is okay to feel whatever you feel
Have no judgement for yourself
Allow any emotions that arise to be felt and
come through

Notice
Observe
Sit with

No rush

Slow all the way down
Lean into spirit
Listen to music that pulls your heartstrings
Move your body
Look for the wonder in life
Breathe in the beauty of a flower
Feel your feet on the ground
Walk intentionally
Sway gently with the rhythm of your heart
Smile to yourself in the mirror
Hug a tree
Cook a nice meal

Make the mundane beautiful

Remember to live life as poetry

Dark goddess

The beast

The Goddess with the hundred heads
With snakes coming out of her hands
the destructive force

We see it outside of us in others
The beast takes the form of your partner, your
parent, your sibling, your friend
It triggers you and pushes you to your edge

You want to slay the beast
You want to defeat it
You want it out

But just for a tiny moment
consider this

Sit with the beast
Maybe even play with the idea of befriending it
Zoom in to have a closer look

Can you see it?
Can you see what it is that you have been afraid
of?

Can you see what it is that you are trying to
eliminate all this time?

The beast is part of you
It is your own power

It is a power that for millennia we have learnt to
be afraid of
Supressed
Avoided
Ignored
And yet, with regard and reverence
It can be moulded into crystalline fire

It is the powerful dark feminine energy
The dark Goddess
She lives in all of us

What would happen if we allowed her to move
in and through our bodies and lives?

Kali

How fearful are you?
Do you understand her?
Do you see her nature?

I have felt her shaking my whole being
I have felt her cascading through my body

I didn't invite her

But she knows when to take over
She knows when it's time to show herself
To be revealed

I only stood there
and experienced her

I voiced her energy
I showed her with my actions

But it wasn't me speaking
it wasn't me doing

It was her stream of consciousness that was
flowing through

Dislodging the smallness
Cleansing the unworthiness
Embracing the sacredness
Becoming part of who I am

Kali

The destroyer of what is not in service anymore

The dark feminine Goddess

This destructive force
has a vast loving heart

She pulsates at the frequency of Love

She's not here to destroy for the sake of
destruction
She's here to destroy for the sake of rebirth
for creation to take place
for the newness to take root
for authenticity to be revealed
for the shadow to be lit up
on fire
to be lit up
with light

Her dualistic nature is essential
it is needed

Her directness is refreshing

When she takes over
the sacred rage of years of suppression
is felt in your bones
It's inevitable
she has to be expressed
You are the medium

If you let her speak through you
the reward is exquisite
Peace
Love
Clarity
are on the other side

One cannot be felt without the other

Let her take over
Don't be fearful

The destruction will be done with the utmost
love

To reconstruct a life around the powerful seed of
you
the authentic you
The you that has always been and always will be
Indestructible

Wrap your life around that part of you
Let all conditioning fall away
Let it peel off your body, your psyche, your life
Let that powerful seed of you
Become the centre of your existence

She's here to do that
Let her
She is part of you
She is you

Oracle

You laugh when I say I am an oracle

You think it is such an outdated word

You have forgotten the power of the Priestess

Now she is only part of a myth

Sitting in the centre of a temple,
smoking and giving out mystic riddles

But here we are
women in modern times
sitting in our kitchens, living rooms, gardens
babies asking for our attention
bosses exchanging our time for money
husbands taking us for granted

Short-sighted society;
cannot see the depth of our existence

Yet here we still are;
our power has not diminished;
despite modern society

The feminine is still awake

We have kept her flame burning
The urge within our bodies is inevitably leading
us

We are forced to keep the feminine urge awake

To sit in the centre of our modern temples
in the midst of our busy lives

And become that ancient oracle
that brings forth

Knowledge
Intuition
Change
Transformation

Against all odds
against all prejudice
against all opinions and judgements

We claim the potency of the word
because we live it

Longing

There is this deep longing in your body
to be held, to be witnessed

Don't dim it down

I know sometimes it hurts

I know you wish it away

But please don't

Hear me out

Hold yourself in this longing
It is there for a reason
It is there to remind you how deeply you care
about life
It is there as your compass if you use it
It is there to show you the way

To a deeper
fulfilling
heart-led
vibrant
creative

life

Don't give your longing away too soon
Don't quench your thirst in finite puddles

Reach for the source
Don't settle for less

The nectar is dripping within your soul
Liquid gold
Awakens your magnificence

Inner war

When the sirens of war blare within you
Choose love

What is more to this three-dimensional existence
If not to love

To live so devoted to self
That your mere existence is a service to the
world

How cliché it all sounds
And how powerfully resonant

How have we downgraded the cliché into boring
Love into fairy-tale
Service into people pleasing
Caring into virtue signalling

How can we live in our deepest private moments
And still choose love

How can we tend to ourselves with such
devotion that our whole life is a service
How can we love ourselves so deeply

that our love spills out and floods the world
around us
Every action to be an expression of love

How so cliché to say
"Make love not war"
But in the helplessness of the task at hand
Is there another solution
But to ask

Where do I still hold war within?

Shadow

Part of the journey
The deep murky waters
The pain
The suffering
It longs for acceptance

Like the ugly sisters in fairy tales

Diving deep into the shadow
brings up dark heavy feelings

We want to avoid
To close in a box in the basement
Out of sight

There was once a man
He put his shadow in a chest and buried it in the
cellar
He spent the rest of his life polishing the cellar
door

But the shadow festers
It will not stop festering
until you accept it

Accept the shadow in its ugliness
in its darkness
Part of the journey
part of who you are

Remember there is no shadow without light
There is an interplay,
a beauty of shadow and light
Creating together shapes and unique
combinations
into one's psyche

Explore the shadow in you

Even maybe
with the excitement of a child looking for
treasure
with the enthusiasm of an adventurer as he sets
out onto his journey
with the love of a mother that holds her child no
matter what

Maybe there is even a possibility to explore your
shadow with joy

Don't leave it buried in the cellar
You are a traveller of the heart
Dive deep into your soul's calling
Be a revolutionary

Letter to my body

Dear body,

I am sorry that once I didn't love you
I am sorry I believed everyone else instead of
you
I am sorry I saw you as something I needed to
fix
I am sorry I have shamed you
I am sorry I allowed others to shame you

I thought you had to be perfect
I thought you ought to be a certain way, a certain
shape

But I know now
You are not meant to be perfect

You are sacred just as you are

You hold in your memory my whole life's
journey
It's been a long journey
To learn to be comfortable in my own skin
It's taken radical self-love
Huge amounts of self-respect

The discomfort of setting boundaries
The pain of saying no
It hasn't always been easy
Far from it

Dear body,

Thank you for moving me through life
Thank you for being the microcosm of life
For always showing me the way
Leading me masterfully to the next step

I know now how to listen to your wisdom
How to trust you deeply
How to decode your messages

I know now that I am meant to hold you in my
arms
To let you shiver when you need to
To comfort you and love you

All of you, every part, every cell

I know now that you are not meant to be perfect
You never were

You are so much more than just perfect

I honour you

I see you
I love you

Pain is the first portal

You got the call
You got the vision

Impatience floods in

You want better now
You want results now
You cannot wait
for the release
for your transformation
for your new life to begin
for abundance
for healing
for your desires to be manifested

But you are jumping ahead
You try to fly before you walk

You think healing means easy
You think you will arrive at the destination
Reach the forever home
But life knows the way

Pain is the first portal

The shaman

The shaman sat me down
I resisted
I didn't want to lie in bed
He said I must
He said I am ready

I followed him
In pain
With resistance
I decided to listen to his higher wisdom

I lied in bed for 3 days and 3 nights
through sweat and tears
through altered states of consciousness
feeling it all
reassuring me that this is needed
there is a reason behind it all
I may not know what it is yet
but it will reveal itself when the time is right

For now I have to trust
For now only faith is my buoy

I soothe the ego
with affirmations of love

with promises of an upgrade

3 days and 3 nights have passed
the pain has subsided
my faith held me afloat

I am ready to see the light

I still don't know why
or what has been achieved

But something has changed
something has shifted

I look at my body with new eyes
I feel my inner world lighter
I try out my new feelings
My new body

And then it is revealed to me

the shaman put me through the portal of pain
the portal to healing
Yet another layer has been shed
Deeper healing has occurred

A rebirth
I am a different person
same but different

more of me
more integration
more wholeness
more aliveness

Don't fear pain
It is a master teacher

Allow the shaman to take you through the hard
rocks
This is your refinement

You are the dove that will fly through them

Trust
trust
trust

Polarity

Wise woman
Awakened to your power
You are his invitation
To rise up
To awaken deeper layers of his soul

Wise man
Awakened to your power
You are her safety
To soften
To drop deeper into the void of creation

Together you create magic

Only if you knew how much magic you can
bring into the world

It brings tears to my eyes
It breaks my heart open
To sense the energy of polarity
To feel the beauty

Let's not keep it as potential
Let's not waste the opportunity to meet each
other

Eye to eye
Heart to heart

Let's make this a reality
Embody the essence of who we are
And together
Holding hands
Feeling each other
Witnessing our homecoming
We change lives

Sisterhood

Holding your hand
not because I have to
only because I want to

I see you
I feel your heart

I know that with my support
we can both flourish

Sisters from the same source

Divine circle
Sacred waters
The priestesses' temple

Why have we forgotten the sister love?
Such balm for the heart
Such force of nature
when we come together

I see your artistry
Your creativity
Your beauty
Your softness and determination

I know the world needs your art

Once someone told you your art is not good
enough
You believed them
You hid your brilliance
You supressed the urge within you to create

Not anymore

There is a way beautiful soul
And it is hiding in all the uncomfortable places

I am here for you
I hold your hand

Never fear again

Are you ready to find your edges and go
beyond?
Will you dare to go there?

One step outside your edges and…

You will be flooded with new energy
Vibrancy will be your state of being
You will be the expression of life

Will you dare live life as the artist you are?

Will you take the call?

I am here for you
I hold your hand

Homecoming

Confused travellers that have forgotten the way
they have forgotten that life is creating
a web of cause and effect
a play of in and out
swirling around and away
detour on detour
up and down

We are all on a journey
All seeking home

But home is where our two feet land
The essence of Hestia always present

She's there to help us return
back to the centre of Self
Back to where home is

She rekindles the fire
She warms our hearts

She reminds us
That our body is our home
Our body is our sanctuary

There is no Ithaca
There is no destination to reach

Coming home is the destination
And life is the journey